ISBN 978-0-365-07783-1
PIBN 11267930

n

rado

ESTIMATING ENGELMANN SPRUCE BEETLE INFESTATIONS IN THE CENTRAL ROCKY MOUNTAINS

By

F. B. Knight,[1] W. F. McCambridge,[2] and B. H. Wilford[1]

INTRODUCTION

The Engelmann spruce beetle (Dendroctonus engelmanni Hopk.) is a primary insect pest of Engelmann spruce in the central Rocky Mountain region. This insect is a bark beetle of the family Scolytidae and is one of the many destructive members of the genus Dendroctonus. The life history, habits, and control of this beetle have been studied in recent years by Massey.[3] In general, the insect has a 2-year life cycle in the central Rocky Mountain region. The first winter is passed in the larval stage in the bole of the tree, the second as an adult beetle. The adult usually hibernates in the base of the tree in which it developed. Attacking beetles (fig. 1D) bore into the bark during June and July and construct vertical egg galleries (fig. 1C) about 6 inches long in the phloem. Eggs are laid in groups (fig. 1A) along the galleries and, after hatching, the larvae (fig. 1B) feed out radially and girdle the tree.

1/ Rocky Mountain Forest and Range Experiment Station, U. S. Department of Agriculture, Forest Service, with central headquarters at Colorado A & M College, Fort Collins, Colorado.

2/ Southeastern Forest Experiment Station, U. S. Department of Agriculture, Forest Service, Asheville, North Carolina.

3/ Massey, C. L. and Wygant, N. D., Biology and Control of the Engelmann Spruce Beetle in Colorado. U. S. Dept. Agr. Circ. 944, 35 pp., illus. 1954.

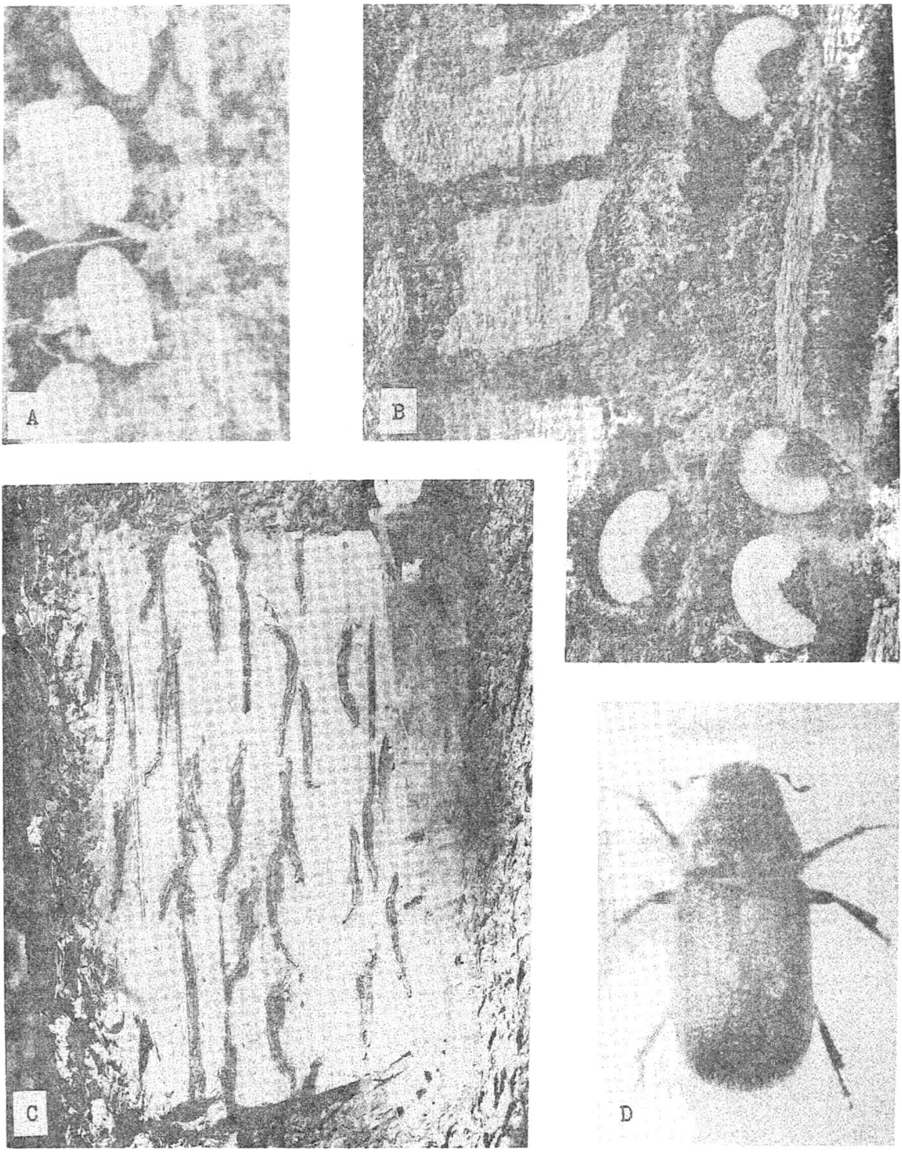

Figure 1.—A, Eggs of the Engelmann spruce beetle. Actual length is approximately 1 mm. B, Engelmann spruce beetle larvae in a bark sample of Engelmann spruce. C, Egg galleries of the Engelmann spruce beetle. D, Adult Engelmann spruce beetle - actual length approximately 1/4 inch.

Newly infested trees are difficult to recognize even at short distances, because pitch tubes at the points of attack generally are very small or absent. Each tree must be inspected carefully around the base for red dust from borings. Engelmann spruce is the primary host of the beetle although lodgepole pine and blue spruce also are attacked when mixed with Engelmann spruce. Although many lodgepole pines die, the insect broods usually do not develop to maturity.

The destruction of Engelmann spruce and lodgepole pine in Colorado amounted to approximately 4.5 billion board-feet in the period from 1939 to 1953 as a result of attacks by this insect. This epidemic developed in the heavy windfall of Engelmann spruce that occurred during 1939 on the Grand Mesa, White River, and Routt National Forests. While protected from their natural enemies, the woodpeckers, by snow that covered the windfall spruce, large populations of insects developed and spread to surrounding green trees. This is typical of the way in which epidemic infestations develop.

To plan and carry out a control project that will check an outbreak, surveys must be made to gain factual information on the infestation. It is of primary importance to determine: (1) The locations of all epidemic areas, (2) reliable estimates of the numbers of infested trees within the epidemic areas, and (3) the general locations of the concentrations of infested trees within each epidemic area. This information must be available well ahead of the control operation so that logistics can be properly carried out.

An evaluation of the amount and kind of natural control factors and an estimation of their effects upon the course of an outbreak is also an integral part of an appraisal survey. Evaluation of these factors is much more complicated than the determination of the location and number of infested trees. The techniques being developed to appraise and forecast these factors will be the subject of subsequent publications.

A survey field crew consists of 3 or 4 men with full camping equipment and a Jeep and trailer for travel into the high spruce country. Usually camp is established in an area for 1 or 2 weeks, then moved to the next area (fig. 2). The camp is set up as closely as possible to the work to reduce travel time by Jeep and on foot to the survey lines.

Figure 2.-- Typical camp of survey crew. Setup is for 1 night or longer, as the survey schedule dictates.

SURVEY METHODS

When a crew commences work in an infestation of unknown magnitude, several conditions must be determined. First, does the infestation warrant an intensive survey? Second, what portion of the area needs an intensive survey? Third, what acreage will be included? The answers to these questions come from careful scrutiny of aerial photographs and scouting of the area on foot or horseback. The purpose of scouting is to find all epidemic areas that need to be systematically covered. Since the entire area of spruce cannot be scouted, the more susceptible spruce stands are determined from photograph interpretations and observations in the field. These susceptible stands are scouted to determine the need for intensive coverage. The susceptibility of spruce stands generally follows this order:

1. Spruce in creekbottoms.
2. Better stands of spruce on benches and high ridges.
3. Poorer stands on benches and high ridges.
4. Mixtures of spruce and lodgepole pine.
5. Stands containing all immature spruce.

If scouting reveals a serious infestation, then systematic ground surveys are planned to:

1. Obtain a reliable estimate of the gross area infested.

2. Obtain an accurate estimate of the number of infested trees in the area.

3. Learn where the infestation concentrations are located.

4. Appraise the natural control forces and their probable effect upon the infestation (techniques for which are not included in this paper).

The system developed for use in the central Rocky Mountains is a 1/10-acre plot cruise method. One man from the party runs each line and tallies data from a series of 1/10-acre circular plots (radius 37.2 feet) along the line usually at 2-chain intervals. The cruiser measures distance by pacing and keeps a straight line by using a hand compass. Intensity of coverage is varied by changing the distance between cruise lines. Location of the first cruise line from the edge of an area is chosen at random. All other lines are systematically spaced.

All the cruise lines should be plotted on photographs (fig. 3) and type maps. In addition, areas of infestation concentration should be shown. This information is very important to the logistical work of the control program, especially in the planning of access roads.

The scope of the infestation is estimated from cruise data, and sampling variances are analyzed to give confidence limits. If the desired accuracy is not obtained, more cruise lines are run.

Although the systematic surveys made in spruce do not have all of the desired qualities of random sampling, confidence limits are computed by analyzing the variances between cruise lines, thus, the individual cruise lines are the sampling units. The weights of the sampling units are the number of 1/10-acre plots in the lines.

The formula used in computing the variance of the mean is as follows:

$$V(\bar{y}) = \frac{S\ (w\ (\ y/w\ )^2\ )\ -\ \bar{y}\ (\ Sy\ )}{(\ n-1\ )\ \ (\ Sw\ )}$$

where:

V = Variance

w = Weight = Number of plots in the cruise line.

y = Number of infested trees in a cruise line.

$\bar{y}$ = Sy/Sw = Number of infested trees per plot.

n = Number of cruise lines in the survey. This number is at least 10, if possible.

A corrected variance is computed. The variance is multiplied by the finite correction, 1 - (percent survey coverage/100).

The confidence interval is computed by multiplying the square root of the corrected variance by a "t" value from a statistical table.

The estimate is computed by multiplying the number of infested trees per plot ($\bar{y}$) by the total possible plots in the survey area (N). The confidence limits are computed by multiplying $SE\bar{y}$ by N. N may be easily computed by multiplying the total acreage by 10.

The 1/10-acre plot was determined to be an efficient size. Larger plots were tested but results were poor because of dense stands. So much time was required to cruise the plots that area coverage was inefficient. Cruise lines with strips of various widths were also tested. Strips as narrow as 1/2 chain were difficult to cruise. Because attacks on spruce do not always completely encircle the bole, all sides of apparently green trees must be checked. This requires a cruiser on strip lines to do two jobs at once, i.e., run a line and pace distance, and examine and pace to all trees off the line. When a cruiser uses a plot system, his attention is on one job at a time.

Figure 3.—— Aerial photograph showing outlined boundary of a survey block and plotted survey lines.

McCambridge[4] compared 1/15- and 1/20-acre plots with 1/10-acre plots to determine whether a more efficient method would result. His study showed that the accuracy of estimates by the three methods was about equal. However, the time required to tally data on the 1/20-acre plot was significantly less than on the 1/10-acre size, as shown in the following tabulation:

Plot Size	Mean Time per Plot
Acres	Minutes
1/10	2.34
1/15	1.96
1/20	1.66

The critical difference between any 2 mean times was computed to be 0.44 minute at the 95 percent level. Thus, the 1/20-acre plot can be cruised significantly faster than the 1/10-acre plot.

From this analysis, it would appear that the 1/20-acre plot might be used to advantage. However, further tests showed that because of time required for travel between plots, offsetting, etc., very little additional line could be run in a day. This, and the fact that in light infestations more zeros (and less reliable estimates and sampling errors) would be tallied with the 1/20-acre plot method, resulted in a decision to retain the 1/10-acre plot method as the standard for surveys in the central Rocky Mountains. The 1/20-acre plot method can be used to advantage in very heavy infestations. Possibly infestations of 10 or more infested trees per acre might be considered as very heavy for this purpose.

Creekbottom infestations present a special problem. The total acreage is often very small and the attacked trees are numerous near the creek but become less numerous as the distance from the creek increases. Usually the total distance from the creek is less than 10 chains and commonly only 2 to 4 chains.

4/ McCambridge, W. F. Special Report FC-1, A Study to Determine the Most Efficient Circular Plot Size for Sampling Engelmann Spruce Stands Infested by the Engelmann Spruce Beetle. Unpublished Report, U. S. Dept. Agr., Bur. Ent. and Plant Quar., Fort Collins, Colorado, 6 pp., 1952.

Cruise lines must be run across the creeks, percent of coverage must be excessively high, and much time is wasted in offsetting. Although creek bottom surveys are expensive, they must be made, and no other successful method has been developed. Luckily, the number of such surveys and their total acreage is generally small.

The current use of ai planes in Engelmann spruce beetle surveys in the central Rocky Mountains is largely limited to reconnaissance, including the delineation of major windthrow areas. At our present stage of technique development, aerial observation cannot be relied upon to detect incipient outbreaks. Once an epidemic is known and has existed for a few years, then the airplane is useful in delineating the overall infestation. The change in color before needles drop from infested trees in Colorado is often quite inconspicuous. Because of this, there must be many infested stems before aerial observers can detect them.

ANALYSIS OF SPRUCE BEETLE SURVEY DATA

The most important factors that affect the amount of error in estimates of the number of beetle-infested trees are: (1) The number of acres, (2) the percent of survey, (3) the number of infested trees, and (4) the distribution of the attacked trees within the stand.

Many blocks of spruce with varying acreages were surveyed in 1950 in the Engelmann spruce beetle outbreak in Colorado. Sampling errors were computed for each block. Some had more error than desirable; others were more accurate than necessary. These errors would be typical of those obtained from surveys of other areas of spruce with similar acreages and infestations. A high proportion of the blocks showed errors within the desired limits of 25 percent at the 2 to 1 level of accuracy.

Since a rough guide was needed to indicate the cruise intensities necessary for surveys of specific blocks, the field data and computed sampling errors for the 1950 survey were utilized in a regression analysis. Ideally, such an analysis should be based on completely random cruise lines. However, the data available are from systematic surveys. The collection of an adequate amount of data from random-type surveys was not economically feasible.

The regression was accomplished by using 119 of the blocks surveyed during 1950. The percentage of coverage varied from 0.56 to 77.50, the acreage from 2 to 5,500, and the infestation rate from 0.44 to 107.30 trees per acre. Several variables and interactions were tested. Those showing significance were:

1. X_1X_2 — The interaction between percent coverage and acreage.

2. X_3 — The infestation rate in trees per acre.

3. X_3^2 — The square of X_3.

By the use of the resulting regression formula and computed values of the coefficients, the value of Y in percent of sampling error was computed for many inserted values of X_1, X_2, and X_3. Tables were developed and curves were plotted for various infestation rates and survey percentages. These tables (1 and 2) and curves have proved to be useful in determining the percentage cruise needed in an area where a specific minimum accuracy is desired.

In 1951, 17 blocks were surveyed in which the tables were used as a basis for the percentage cruise. The infestation rate to use in entering the table was determined roughly from scouting. Only 4 of the 17 sampling errors did not fall within the predicted ranges of sampling errors from the curves. This is a little better than should be expected for the 2 to 1 level of accuracy.

On individual blocks, the desired accuracy (economically justifiable) is around 25 percent. Table 1 shows the percentages of coverage required for various acreages and infestation rates to obtain 25-percent allowable error. The values were computed with the regression formula.

Table 1.--Percent of sample coverage necessary in areas of various sizes, for allowable error of 25 percent, confidence at the 2 to 1 level.1/

Number of infested trees per acre	Area of infestation in acres					
	200	500	1,000	2,500	5,000	10,000
	Percent					
1	33.0	13.5	7.0	3.0	1.5	1.0
5	27.0	11.0	5.5	2.5	1.5	1.0
10	20.0	8.0	4.0	2.0	1.0	0.5
20	8.0	3.5	2.0	1.0	0.5	0.5

1/ Percent of sample coverage rounded to next higher 0.5 percent.

ing many blocks) better than 25-percent accuracy is desired and expected. Table 2 shows the percentages of coverages needed for obtaining estimates with 10-percent allowable error.

Table 2.--Percent of sample coverage necessary in areas of various sizes, for allowable error of 10 percent, confidence at the 2 to 1 level.1/

Number of infested trees per acre	Area of infestation in acres					
	200	500	1,000	2,500	5,000	10,000
	- - - - - - - - Percent - - - - - - - -					
1	57.0	23.0	11.5	5.0	2.5	1.5
5	51.0	20.5	10.5	4.5	2.5	1.5
10	44.0	18.0	9.0	4.0	2.0	1.0
20	32.5	13.0	6.5	3.0	1.5	1.0
30	23.0	9.5	5.0	2.0	1.0	0.5
40	16.5	6.5	3.5	1.5	1.0	0.5

1/ Percent of sample coverage rounded to next higher 0.5 percent.

SUMMARY

Estimates of Engelmann spruce beetle infestations in the central Rocky Mountains are accomplished by systematic ground coverage of the areas involved. Data are tallied from 1/10-acre circular plots at 2-chain intervals along parallel cruise lines. The distance between lines is varied to obtain the desired percentage of survey.

This 1/10-acre plot method has been compared in the field with both larger and smaller plots and with strips of various widths. It was found that the 1/20-acre plot can be used to advantage in areas containing very heavy infestations. The methods using plots larger than 1/10 acre and the strip methods gave less accurate results than the 1/10-acre plot method.

A regression analysis on factors affecting the accuracy of the 1/10-acre plot method showed that the percentage of coverage, acreage, and number of trees infested per acre significantly affect the sampling error of a survey. Tables were developed from the regression to show the percentage of coverage needed to obtain the desired accuracy. These have been used successfully as a guide for sampling intensity in the field.

In order that a useful guide could be developed for field use, a realistic interpretation of randomness was accepted. The major requirement was met, since all parts of the survey area were equally likely to be crossed by a cruise line. Although the analyses were not on data that fitted all requirements of random samples, the results have been applicable to the problems in the field.

Agriculture—Colo A&M, Ft. Collins

CPSIA information can be obtained
at www.ICGtesting.com
Printed in the USA
BVHW070323290119
538842BV00036B/4651/P

9 780365 077831